Alive in the WORD

LITURGICAL SEASONS

EASTER

Season of Realized Hope

Catherine Upchurch

Little Rock Scripture Study

LITURGICAL PRESS
Collegeville, Minnesota

www.littlerockscripture.org

Nihil obstat: Rev. Robert Harren, J.C.L., *Censor Deputatus*.
Imprimatur: ✠ Most Rev. Donald J. Kettler, J.C.L., D.D., Bishop of St. Cloud, September 3, 2021.

Cover design by Ann Blattner. Cover photo: Getty Images. Used with permission.

Photos/illustrations: Pages 8, 11, 13, 17, 24, 28, 29, 30, 34, 38, 42, Getty Images; page 20, Lightstock; page 36, Clifford M. Yeary. Used with permission.

ISBN: 978-0-8146-6614-2 978-0-8146-6638-8 (ebook)

Contents

Introduction

Alive in the Word brings you resources to deepen your understanding of Scripture, offer meaning for your life today, and help you to pray and act in response to God's word.

Use any volume of **Alive in the Word** in the way best suited to you.

- **For individual learning and reflection**, consider this an invitation to prayerfully journal in response to the questions you find along the way. And be prepared to move from head to heart and then to action.
- **For group learning and reflection**, arrange for three sessions where you will use the material provided as the basis for faith sharing and prayer. You may ask group members to read each chapter in advance and come prepared with questions answered. In this kind of session, plan to be together for about an hour. Or, if your group prefers, read and respond to the questions together without advance preparation. With this approach, it's helpful to plan on spending more time for each group session in order to adequately work through each of the chapters.

- **For a parish-wide event or use within a larger group,** provide each person with a copy of this volume, and allow time during the event for quiet reading, group discussion and prayer, and then a final commitment by each person to some simple action in response to what he or she learned.

This volume on the topic of Easter is one of several volumes that explore **Liturgical Seasons.** Our church accents seasons within each year that allow us to enter into the story of salvation. This is commonly referred to as the liturgical calendar. Its purpose is not to mark the passage of time but to understand the overall mystery of salvation in Jesus Christ, from his incarnation and birth through his ministry, death, resurrection, and sending of the Spirit. By meditating on the themes of these various seasons in the church year, we are more fully able to live the mystery of Christ in our own lives.

Prologue

"[A]s the first day of the week was dawning . . ." (Matt 28:1)

"Very early when the sun had risen, on the first day of the week . . ." (Mark 16:2)

"[A]t daybreak on the first day of the week . . ." (Luke 24:1)

"On the first day of the week . . ." (John 20:1)

From the earliest times, Christians recognized that Jesus' resurrection changed the world. They chose the day of his rising from the dead, the first day of the week, to celebrate the continuing presence of Jesus in their midst. It is as if every Sunday is Easter, set aside to confirm that because Jesus lives, so do we.

As followers of Christ, we can benefit from meditating on the events of Easter and considering the ways the risen Lord lives in us and through us. We are better able to cultivate an Easter spirituality—a conviction of hope in the face of sorrow—by studying and praying with New Testament texts that recount the empty tomb, describe encounters with the risen Christ, and explain what these realities mean for us. In this book we will explore three of these texts: two from the gospels and one from Paul's letters.

Easter is a season that anchors us in hope, not wishful thinking. We hear the witness of believers who are like us: seeking, questioning, and wondering. In their witness to the risen Jesus, we realize that we do not have to look very far or have every question answered. Each sign of new life in our world flows from an investment in the kind of life that Jesus embraced, before the tomb and after it. This is the cause for our hope. Christ is truly risen!

He Has Been Raised

> *Begin by asking God to assist you in your prayer and study. Then read Matthew 28:1-10, an encounter with the risen Christ.*

Matthew 28:1-10
[1]After the sabbath, as the first day of the week was dawning,
Mary Magdalene and the other Mary came to see the tomb.
[2]And behold, there was a great earthquake; for an angel of
the Lord descended from heaven, approached, rolled back
the stone, and sat upon it. [3]His appearance was like lightning
and his clothing was white as snow. [4]The guards were shaken
with fear of him and became like dead men. [5]Then the angel
said to the women in reply, "Do not be afraid! I know that

you are seeking Jesus the
crucified. [6]He is not here,
for he has been raised
just as he said. Come
and see the place where
he lay. [7]Then go quickly
and tell his disciples, 'He
has been raised from the
dead, and he is going be-
fore you to Galilee; there
you will see him.' Behold,

I have told you." [8]Then they went away quickly from the tomb, fearful yet overjoyed, and ran to announce this to his disciples. [9]And behold, Jesus met them on their way and greeted them. They approached, embraced his feet, and did him homage. [10]Then Jesus said to them, "Do not be afraid. Go tell my brothers to go to Galilee, and there they will see me."

> *After a few moments of quiet reflection, consider the background information found in "Setting the Scene." This information will help you put the passage in context.*

Setting the Scene

The word "gospel" comes from the Greek *evangelion*, which means "good news" or "good tidings." Jesus is the incarnation of God's Good News for the world, and the four gospels announce the Good News of Jesus to communities with slightly different backgrounds and needs. The purpose of a gospel is to invite listeners to encounter Jesus and to follow him.

In each of the gospels, we find stories about the resurrection of Jesus (Matt 28; Mark 16; Luke 24; and John 20–21). The details vary somewhat, but none of the gospels describe the resurrection itself. Instead, these accounts describe the empty tomb of Jesus, giving witness that something unique has happened. And in each gospel, the risen Jesus eventually appears to his followers. That time between finding the empty tomb and encountering Christ himself is where the struggle between doubt and hope plays out most dramatically. This happens for Jesus' disciples in every generation.

Matthew's resurrection account involves five scenes, two of which actually occur before the resurrection. In the first scene (27:57-61), Joseph of Arimathea requests the body of Jesus, lays it in his own tomb, and seals it with a large stone. In the second (27:62-66), the Jewish leaders request that Pilate place guards at the tomb to ensure that the body of Jesus will not be stolen. Jesus was known to have said his body would be raised in three days, so they did not want any possibility of trickery. In the third scene (28:1-10), which we will explore in detail, two women come to the tomb, discover it empty, are told by an angel that Jesus has been raised, and then encounter the risen Christ. In the fourth (28:11-15), the guards are bribed by the Jewish elders to say that Jesus' body was stolen while they slept. And in the final scene (28:16-20), the risen Jesus appears to the disciples gathered in Galilee and commissions them to make disciples of all nations, assuring them that he is with them always.

Matthew 28:1-10 will now be considered a few verses at a time. Questions in the margins may be used for personal reflection, journaling, or group discussion.

Understanding the Scene Itself

1 After the sabbath, as the first day of the week was dawning, Mary Magdalene and the other Mary came to see the tomb.

In Matthew's account of the crucifixion of Jesus, we are told that "many women" who had followed Jesus from Galilee were faithfully present at the cross. But only two women are named: Mary Magdalene and "Mary the mother of James and Joseph" (27:55-56). While this is Mary Magdalene's first appearance in the Gospel of Matthew, we know of her from an account in Luke 8:1-3, where Jesus is said to have cured her of evil spirits and restored her to health. Mary the mother of James and Joseph is presumed to be "the other Mary" mentioned both at the burial of Jesus (27:61) and here with Mary Magdalene, as the two women approach the tomb on the first day of the week (28:1).

The story of the women coming to the tomb provides witnesses to the resurrection events. Their coming also demonstrates the power of loving witness to the death of a loved one. What are some of the ways we honor those we love who have died?

In other accounts of women coming to the tomb of Jesus, they are reported to be there to anoint his body (Mark 16:1; Luke 23:55–24:1). But in Matthew's account, an earlier anointing of Jesus takes the place of the anointing at the tomb. This anointing occurred in Bethany at the house of Simon the leper, just a few days before Passover and the arrest of Jesus. There, a woman poured a jar of costly perfumed oil over Jesus' head, much to the dismay and objections of the disciples (26:6-13). Jesus used the moment to tell his disciples that she was preparing him for burial and that her action would always be remembered.

Readers of Matthew's gospel today cannot help but notice that it is three women who pay Jesus the homage that is the only fitting tribute to his sacrificial love—the woman who anointed him, Mary Magdalene, and "the other Mary." These faithful followers of Jesus possess a level of understanding that is still eluding the likes of Peter, James, John, and the other apostles. Jesus' ministry consistently embraces those who are discounted by society. How appropriate that the ones who stand by him in this dire time are those ordinarily overlooked or even shunned by others!

When have you realized some spiritual truth from an unexpected person, someone you may have bypassed in usual circumstances?

[2]And behold, there was a great earthquake; for an angel of the Lord descended from heaven, approached, rolled back the stone, and sat upon it. [3]His appearance was like lightning and his clothing was white as snow. [4]The guards were shaken with fear of him and became like dead men.

The description of an Easter earthquake is unique to Matthew's account, as is the earthquake that earlier accompanied Jesus' death (27:51-52). Matthew wants his audience to connect the death and resurrection of Jesus with Old Testament theophanies, or manifestations of God. In this gospel, earthquakes—earlier described as the "beginning of the labor pains" (see Jesus' words at 24:7-8)—are expected to usher in the fullness of God's kingdom. Just as the earth labors in storms, earthquakes, tornadoes, and floods, creating new pathways and surfaces,

God labors to bring about a new reality through his Son's life, death, and resurrection.

When have you seen the power of natural events, even dangerous or disastrous ones, reshape understandings about God or the power of community?

Matthew includes further evidence of God's intervention in the appearance of "an angel of the Lord" at the tomb of Jesus. Just as an angel assured Joseph that Mary's pregnancy was the result of divine intervention (1:18-21) and then appeared again to protect the infant Jesus and his family from the murderous plans of Herod (2:13-15), God's messenger now appears to the women at the tomb.

The gem in these verses is the reaction of the guards who "were shaken with fear of him and became like dead men." The guards are present at the tomb as a sign of imperial power, presumed by many to be absolute. Jesus, even a crucified and buried Jesus, is seen as a threat to the power structure of his day. As an appointee of the Roman emperor, Pilate's job is to preserve law and order and to quash any possibility of threats, not only to the emperor's position, but also to the status quo. Rather than standing courageously

Later in Matthew, the guards will be bribed to say that Jesus' body must have been stolen while they were sleeping (28:11-15). Why is it sometimes easier to avoid the truth than to do the hard work of wrestling with what the truth means for us?

by the tomb, the guards crumple in fear, utterly paralyzed. On the verge of revealing that Jesus is risen from the dead, the text first tells us that it is the guards who are in the grip of death! By extension, the presumed absolutism of imperial power is dying.

[5]Then the angel said to the women in reply, "Do
not be afraid! I know that you are seeking Jesus
the crucified. [6]He is not here, for he has been
raised just as he said. Come and see the place
where he lay. [7]Then go quickly and tell his dis-
ciples, 'He has been raised from the dead, and he
is going before you to Galilee; there you will see
him.' Behold, I have told you." [8]Then they went
away quickly from the tomb, fearful yet over-
joyed, and ran to announce this to his disciples.

The angel's proclamation, "Do not be afraid!" stands in stark contrast to the guards' fear, and even the fear of death itself. While it is perfectly normal to respond in fear to dangerous or even confusing situations, we do not have to live in fear or be defined by it. In fact, fear can become a signal that it is time to rely on the sure and powerful presence of God. God's messenger is offering assurance that, in Jesus, God is still present and will always be with us. It is an echo of the divine assurance that came at the beginning of the Gospel of Matthew when Jesus was named Emmanuel, which means "God is with us" (1:23-24), an assurance that will repeat at the close of the gospel in Jesus' words to his followers: "I am with you always, until the end of the age" (28:20).

How do you deal with the fears that arise in your daily life? And the bigger fears that you may have for those you love? Is it helpful to know that the message to "fear not" appears close to 400 times in the Bible?

The angel acknowledges that the women are seeking "Jesus the crucified." The original Greek phrasing here makes use of what grammarians call a perfect participle. In this context it recognizes that a past action (the crucifixion of Jesus) has relevance in the present. In other words, while it is true that Jesus was crucified at a point in time, the phrasing translated as "Jesus the crucified" communicates that the reality of his crucifixion is ongoing. Even in his risen state, Jesus bears the wounds of his suffering and death. Interestingly, the wounds of Jesus are elsewhere used as proof that he is the Jesus his followers have come to know (see John 20:19-27). Perhaps as important is the knowledge that, in carrying the wounds of his crucifixion, the risen Lord carries the wounds of the world and the promise of healing.

Jesus becomes, as we all do, the product of his life experiences and God's life in him. He does not simply rise from the dead and shed the human life he led. He is raised bodily, wounds and all. When you consider the wounds you carry (as well as wounds you may have caused), does this give you hope? How so?

Verse 6 contains three quick moments. First, the angel says simply, "He is not here." Empty of its power to contain the Lord of life, the physical tomb no longer contains the body of Jesus. Second, the angel says that Jesus "has been raised

Jesus' disciples were mired in grief rather than open to joy. How does this pattern play itself out in our own lives and in our own time? What are some ways we can break out of this pattern?

just as he said." Jesus had predicted his passion and resurrection several times before his death (Matt 16:21; 17:22-23; 20:17-19). Following each of these predictions, Jesus' followers expressed resistance, grief, or lack of understanding, indicating that their focus was on the suffering to come rather than the promise of resurrection, which they clearly did not grasp. Finally the angel says, "Come and see the place where he lay." Throughout his ministry, Jesus understood the power of giving witness in a way that people could see, taste, or hear. Indeed, from the beginning of history, God has used our senses to reveal what divinity looks like, and in the person of Jesus it always looks like life. Seeing an empty tomb with one's own eyes could produce doubt, or it could produce hope. All these centuries later, with the benefit of hindsight and insight, believing in the witness of Mary Magdalene and the other Mary, we dare to hope in things seen and unseen, in the disruption of evil, and in the promise of life even in the midst of suffering.

Are there places that you associate with coming to know Christ in your own life? Are there times when you return physically or mentally to those places to renew and deepen your experience of Christ?

The angel's instruction challenges the women to shift their focus from the empty tomb to the region of Galilee. This is the place where they first encountered Jesus and, along with others called away from their occupations, began to follow him. They will now return to the place of their calling to share the Good News, to join others in their joy, and to rediscover Jesus in fullness of life.

9And behold, Jesus met them on their way and greeted them. They approached, embraced his

feet, and did him homage. [10]Then Jesus said to them, "Do not be afraid. Go tell my brothers to go to Galilee, and there they will see me."

On the way to Galilee, the risen Jesus himself is fully present to the women. The fact that they can embrace his feet tells us that he is real. Jesus is tangible to them; he has not remained in the grip of death. His very appearance to these women is a sign that he recognizes their fidelity to him in his darkest time. The scene also tells us that the women spontaneously know to reverence the risen Jesus, the author and bearer of new life.

While we may not be able to embrace the feet of Jesus on the dusty roads of Israel, we do have opportunities to reverence Jesus with us every day. What are some of the ways that you honor the risen Christ walking with you in daily living?

The message of the angel at the tomb now comes from the lips of the risen Lord. Like Mary Magdalene in John 20:11-18, the women have been given a commission; they have been sent. They are now apostles in the purest sense of the word, having been sent by God to spread the Good News that death has no power over the Son of God and will ultimately have no power over those who belong to him.

Praying the Word / Sacred Reading

One way to pray with a scene from Scripture is to place yourself in the scene and imagine yourself as one of the characters. In this way, rather than looking at the scene as a whole and already knowing how it will unfold, you can take your place in the scene and allow the events to unfold naturally.

Imagine yourself in the scene of Matthew 28:1-10, the passage we have been studying. After a few moments of allowing the scene to unfold and the characters to come to life, ask God to fill you with the joy that the resurrection surely demands. You may use your own words, or pray the following:

God of life, God who conquers death and fear,
you allow us to move from doubt to trust, from confusion to confidence.
When we find only emptiness, help us to look for your messengers
who will lead us to the places where we first came to know you.
When we experience confusion, come to meet us on our way
and renew in us the hope that is anchored in your undying love.
God of life, make us people of life!

Living the Word

The guards and the women had very different responses to the empty tomb. Perhaps the guards were predisposed to fear and dread because of their position in service to the power of Rome and their fear of the consequences of a missing body. While we know the guards were initially stunned, we do not know how or if their lives might have been transformed in the long term. The women, however, had been following Jesus, listening to his words, witnessing his interactions, and soaking up the will and love of God that he embodied. They were predisposed by their experiences and formation to have the capacity for wonder, hope, and joy.

Easter provides us with the opportunity to rediscover what we have allowed to form and shape us. Are we being formed to expect the unexpected? To receive good news with joy? To allow new life to be the gift we leave with others?

Were Not Our Hearts Burning within Us?

Begin by asking God to assist you in your prayer and study. Then read Luke 24:13-35, an account of a post-resurrection appearance of Jesus.

Luke 24:13-35

13Now that very day two of them were going to a village seven
miles from Jerusalem called Emmaus, 14and they were con-
versing about all the things that had occurred. 15And it hap-
pened that while they were conversing and debating, Jesus
himself drew near and walked with them, 16but their eyes
were prevented from recognizing him. 17He asked them,
"What are you discussing as you walk along?" They stopped,
looking downcast. 18One of them, named Cleopas, said to
him in reply, "Are you the only visitor to Jerusalem who does
not know of the things that have taken place there in these
days?" 19And he replied to them, "What sort of things?" They
said to him, "The things that happened to Jesus the Nazarene,
who was a prophet mighty in deed and word before God and
all the people, 20how our chief priests and rulers both handed
him over to a sentence of death and crucified him. 21But we

were hoping that he would be the one to redeem
Israel; and besides all this, it is now the third day
since this took place. 22Some women from our
group, however, have astounded us: they were
at the tomb early in the morning 23and did not
find his body; they came back and reported that
they had indeed seen a vision of angels who an-
nounced that he was alive. 24Then some of those
with us went to the tomb and found things just
as the women had described, but him they did
not see." 25And he said to them, "Oh, how fool-
ish you are! How slow of heart to believe all that
the prophets spoke! 26Was it not necessary that
the Messiah should suffer these things and enter
into his glory?" 27Then beginning with Moses
and all the prophets, he interpreted to them
what referred to him in all the scriptures. 28As
they approached the village to which they were
going, he gave the impression that he was going
on farther. 29But they urged him, "Stay with us,
for it is nearly evening and the day is almost
over." So he went in to stay with them. 30And it
happened that, while he was with them at table,
he took bread, said the blessing, broke it, and
gave it to them. 31With that their eyes were
opened and they recognized him, but he van-
ished from their sight. 32Then they said to each
other, "Were not our hearts burning [within us]
while he spoke to us on the way and opened the
scriptures to us?" 33So they set out at once and
returned to Jerusalem where they found gath-
ered together the eleven and those with them
34who were saying, "The Lord has truly been
raised and has appeared to Simon!" 35Then the

two recounted what had taken place on the way and how he was made known to them in the breaking of the bread.

After a few moments of quiet reflection on the Emmaus story, consider the background information found in "Setting the Scene." This information will help you put the passage in context.

Setting the Scene

Both the Gospel of Luke and the Acts of the Apostles were written by the same author. Both books mention a certain "Theophilus" in their opening verses. Both contain a prominent travel narrative: in the Gospel of Luke, Jesus and his followers journey from the region of Galilee to Jerusalem; in Acts, Jesus' followers continue the journey by moving out from Jerusalem to the ends of the earth. The "hinge" for these two journeys is the city of Jerusalem: the location of the temple and high holy days sacred to all Jews, the site of Jesus' death and burial, and the place of his resurrection. In Jerusalem one phase of the journey ends, and the other phase begins.

Examine Luke 24:1-12 and Matthew 28:1-10 side by side. What details differ? What do the accounts share in common?

The scene we will explore is found in the final chapter of the Gospel of Luke and occurs after the women from Galilee discover an empty tomb and are told that Jesus has been raised. Luke's version of the empty tomb (24:1-12) contains slightly different details than Matthew's version, including the observation that the story told by the women "seemed like nonsense" to the apostles. In Luke's account, Peter runs to the tomb to confirm their report and goes back to the others feeling "amazed." At this point, we are left wondering if the disciples comprehend what has happened to Jesus. That sense of being unsure is addressed beautifully in the next scene as two of Jesus' followers head toward Emmaus.

> *Because this passage is lengthy and space is limited, please refer back to the account on pages 20–22 as we explore the passage several verses at a time. Continue using the questions in the margins for your own reflection or group discussion.*

Understanding the Scene Itself

See 24:13-18.

The passage begins with a reference to "that very day," presumably three days after the death and burial of Jesus—the day the tomb is discovered empty, the day the women of Galilee receive the startling news that Jesus has been raised. "That very day," according to Luke, is the day that Peter runs to the tomb upon hearing the news to see with his own eyes that the body of Jesus is gone (24:12). "That very day," while not a day of tragedy, is still a day that does not yet make sense. Speculation and debate is no doubt on the lips of many in Jerusalem and is on the lips of two of Jesus' followers who are making their way out of town.

Can you think of significant events that you recall by remembering what you were doing at that time? In this way, do you feel more connected to that larger event? Does it tend to live within you longer?

Why these two disciples are leaving Jerusalem is unclear. Could they be disheartened and want to distance themselves from their dashed hopes? Could they be fearful of suffering the same fate

as Jesus? Could they merely be on their way back to their families? We do not know why they are traveling, but we do know that they are intently "conversing and debating" (v. 15) as they walk along. They are trying to make sense of what they witnessed in Jesus' dying and of what they heard about his rising. They are on the way to a small town that has been lost to history, and, at the same time, they are on their way to a depth of understanding that will never be lost.

In almost all of the resurrection appearances of Jesus, initially he is not recognized. In this account from Luke, it is said of the two disciples that "their eyes were prevented from recognizing him" (v. 16). Jesus is not a ghost or a smelly corpse meant to frighten them. He is a man, flesh and bones, joining their conversation and their journey. Are they so shattered about the events of the previous day that they cannot see him right beside them? Are they so wrapped up in their discussion and attempts to make sense of it all that they miss his true identity? Or are their minds and hearts just not quite ready for that moment of recognition? Do they need the time to recall more clearly what Jesus told them along the way, how he tried to prepare them?

When the yet-unrecognized Jesus asks them what they are discussing, they ask if he is the only visitor to Jerusalem who does not know what's been happening. They cannot believe that the rumors of Jesus' broken body disappearing from the tomb have not reached the ears of this fellow traveler. Ironically, these disciples are the ones who cannot see the evidence right before their eyes: the flesh-and-blood evidence that Jesus is alive, raised from the dead.

The disciples of Jesus were hesitant to believe in the resurrection even though Jesus had tried to prepare them. We may share some of their hesitation. Why do you think such Good News is sometimes hard to accept?

See 24:19-21.

Verses 19 and 20 provide a quick, powerful summary of who Jesus was and how his identity threatened those in power. First, the travelers essentially describe Jesus as being "one of us" by referring to him as a "Nazarene." Jesus had a family and a personal history in Nazareth. Long before he was known as a prophet, he was simply a Jewish boy who grew up in a small town in northern Galilee. It was in Nazareth that the angel appeared to Mary and revealed what God had in store for her and the child she would bear (Luke 1:26-38). It was in Nazareth that Jesus was prepared for his future, where he "grew and became strong, filled with wisdom; and the favor of God was upon him" (2:40).

Where are the places you associate with providing your formation? And who are the people that God used to shape who you have become and are becoming still?

The second piece of Jesus' identity is found in the phrase "a prophet mighty in deed and word before God and all the people" (v. 19). This is not the first time this language has appeared in Luke's account. Earlier in the gospel, Jesus proclaimed a passage from the prophet Isaiah in his hometown synagogue. His claim that Isaiah's words were being fulfilled in him caused the people to react with both wonder and skepticism (4:16-24). Jesus' response that "no prophet is accepted in his own native place" underscores his prophetic role and has since become a way of explaining rejection by those who know us best.

A reference to Jesus' prophetic role appears again about halfway through the Gospel of Luke. As Jesus made his way to Jerusalem, tensions were rising between him and the powers of the day. Herod wanted him dead, and when Jesus was warned to leave by those who were concerned for his safety, he reminded them that Jerusalem was his destiny: "[I]t is impossible that a prophet should die outside of Jerusalem" (13:31-33). By the time of his death and the discovery of his empty tomb, Jesus' followers are beginning to understand. Like Moses, who knew God "face to face" (Deut 34:10), and Jeremiah, whose preaching put him in danger of being killed (Jer 26:7-19), Jesus fulfills a prophetic role for God's people. He speaks with the authority of God, and he preaches reform and repentance.

Jesus' prophetic witness, however, is not yet fully realized by the two disciples. They are wrapped up in their own disappointment: "[W]e were hoping that he would be the one to redeem Israel" (v. 21). The public suffering and humiliation of the cross has tampered with their trust in

Israel's prophets are not fortune-tellers. They speak from the heart of God, dismantling injustice and building up a covenant people.

God and their belief that Jesus is God's Anointed. Why? Because they still do not understand that their notions about God's Anointed One might be getting in the way of accepting the new and wonderful thing God is doing in their midst.

The discouragement of Jesus' followers as they leave Jerusalem is not so unlike our own disillusionments. We carry within us preconceived ideas about how God will or should act on our behalf. Our hopes are sometimes so attached to our own limited view of reality that we fail to hope in what God has promised or to believe in the surprising ways that God can accomplish in us and for us what he has promised.

Recall a time when you felt confused or disappointed, when you felt that God had not come through for you. What helped you view this differently? How did you discover something new that God was accomplishing?

The two disciples on the road to Emmaus hoped that Jesus would be the one to bring redemption, perhaps believing that he would deliver Israel from Roman occupation or reform the leadership in the temple or synagogues. Instead, Jesus died and was buried, and their hopes are suffering the same fate. Jesus could have simply revealed his identity right away, putting

their despair to rest. Instead, he meets them in their despair, determined to journey with them, both physically and spiritually.

See 24:22-26.

Effective teachers and evangelizers look for moments when they can enter into another person's experience. It's a bit like jumping rope—watching for the rhythm of the rope being turned over and over, waiting to jump in at just the right moment. Verses 22-26 describe that moment Jesus has been watching and listening for, the moment he can turn the conversation on its head and reveal in full what the two travelers up to this point knew only in part.

The disciples have just presented the very evidence that could lead to realization and recognition: the women found an empty tomb, they encountered angels who revealed that Jesus was alive, and some of the other disciples confirmed their experience. "[B]ut him they did not see"

(v. 24)—indeed! In Luke's account, the women who went to the tomb did not see him, the other disciples who visited the tomb did not see him, and now the travelers do not see him even as he walks right beside them.

During his ministry, Jesus had tried to tell his followers that he would suffer, but this prediction was shocking in many ways. Despite passages in the psalms and prophets about a suffering messiah, Judaism at the time included no clear expectation of suffering for God's Anointed. Jesus' provocative question in verse 26 ("Was it not necessary that the Messiah should suffer these things and enter into his glory?") sets the stage for the Easter revelation to come.

"Seeing" is often referenced in the gospels as a way of talking about spiritual insight. When you have missed "seeing" the risen Lord in your own life? What stood in your way? A lack of attention, misdirected hopes, or something else altogether? How do you pray for spiritual insight?

See 24:27-29.

None of what Jesus tells the traveling disciples would have been new to them. They were undoubtedly faithful Jews who were familiar with the writings and teachings we now refer to as the

How has studying and praying with the Bible allowed you to discover new dimensions of a Scripture passage? Can you think of a specific example? Are your earlier understandings of Jesus also expanding?

Old Testament. What is new is the way they are hearing their sacred texts as if for the first time.

Scripture remains fresh and alive in our communities because it is breathed into by God (the basic meaning of *divine inspiration*). It addresses universal life experiences across time and cultures, and we bring to it our own life experiences. We live in dialogue with Scripture—the sacred words inform and shape us, and our experiences continuously raise new questions and increase our awareness of God's presence in our midst.

See 24:30-35.

Given our understanding of the full presence of Jesus in our eucharistic celebrations, it is little wonder that verses 30-32 usually captivate us in our reading of the Emmaus account. Jesus is invited to stay with the disciples as their guest upon reaching their destination. But suddenly, without explanation, the guest becomes the host. Jesus' actions at the meal—taking, blessing, breaking, and giving bread—echo Luke's accounts of Jesus

feeding the multitude (9:16) and sharing the Passover meal with his closest followers on the night before he died. "This is my body, which will be given for you," he had told them (22:19). And now they know with clarity that Jesus is alive, present in their sharing.

When have sound teaching and faithful companionship prepared you to realize something deeper in your journey of faith? How does the proclamation of God's Word prepare you to recognize Jesus present in the Eucharist?

On their way to Emmaus, the two travelers had eyes that could not see Jesus and hearts that were unable to recognize his undying love for them. In contrast, their eyes are now opened, and their hearts are burning within them. Even as Jesus vanishes from their sight, he is nearer to them than ever before. What happened along the way? Jesus happened. New life happened.

Jesus went to the travelers, meeting them where they were, even as they walked away from where he had been. Jesus met them in their confusion and listened to them. He fed them with his words and with his actions. He allowed them to move at their own pace, to slowly realize his fully resurrected and real presence.

These two disciples had left Jerusalem because they had not experienced what they expected; now they return to Jerusalem after experiencing what they did not expect. They left in confusion and return in conviction. They left in despair and return in joyful hope. They left in doubt that Jesus was risen and return having met him face to face. They return with a sure sense of their own call to continue the mission of Jesus. As they, the eleven apostles, and other disciples still in Jerusalem share stories of their encounters with the risen Lord, they are all becoming more than a group of ragtag believers who are confused and at lost ends. They are becoming the church.

At World Youth Day 2013, Pope Francis embraced this vision of a church that continues to accompany its members just as Jesus accompanied his disciples on the road to Emmaus:

> [W]e need a church capable of walking at people's side, of doing more than simply listening to them; a church that accompanies them on their journey; a church able to make sense of the "night" contained in the flight of so many of our brothers and sisters from Jerusalem; a church that realizes that the reasons why people leave also contain reasons why they can eventually return. But we need to know how to interpret, with courage, the larger picture. Jesus warmed the hearts of the disciples of Emmaus. (Address of Pope Francis to the Bishops of Brazil, July 2013)

Pope Francis often speaks of the power of creating a culture of encounter and accompaniment. This is the basic human task of forming relationships. How might we as individuals and as parish communities become more attuned to those moments that are open for deeper conversations?

Praying the Word / Sacred Reading

Find a quiet place where you can read the Emmaus story again. Allow the quiet to lead you to words of prayer, your own or words such as these:

We are travelers, Lord, and sometimes we simply feel lost as we put one foot in front of the other, ever onward, but to what? Provide companions as we journey, and lead us together to surprising places where we will encounter you . . .

Ordinary places,
Overlooked places.
Along the way, teach us to hear your words with a fresh awareness of their meaning, unafraid to stop and breathe "Aha!" when we hear a new dimension of your voice. Even after all these years of hearing the stories of faith, surprise us . . .
With burning hearts,
With a change of heart.
And when we know without doubt that you are near, that you are alive in our midst, help us to treasure your presence, not as a possession, but as a gift to be shared. Direct our feet back to familiar places and then on to new horizons . . .
Become our compass, our true north.
Announce your Good News through us.
Make of our lives a pilgrimage of trusting that you are with us.

Living the Word

At this time, bring to Jesus whatever in your life is tempting you to walk away from an empty tomb, a place that gives testimony that Jesus is alive but leaves you perplexed and even doubtful. Seek out a fellow believer who can share this burden with you and can walk with you until you recognize Jesus' presence with you, or be that companion to someone else who is struggling with being disillusioned or feeling abandoned. Together, take advantage of receiving the Eucharist. Praying with your brokenness will help you to recognize Jesus in the breaking of the bread.

Christ the Firstfruits

Take a few moments to ask God to assist you in your prayer and study. Then read 1 Corinthians 15:20-28, a portion of Paul's letter to a community grappling with what the resurrection meant to them.

1 Corinthians 15:20-28

20 But now Christ has been raised from the dead, the firstfruits
of those who have fallen asleep. 21 For since death came
through a human being, the resurrection of the dead came
also through a human being. 22 For just as in Adam all die, so
too in Christ shall all be brought to life, 23 but each one in
proper order: Christ the firstfruits; then, at his coming, those
who belong to Christ; 24 then comes the end, when he hands
over the kingdom to his God and Father, when he has

destroyed every sovereignty and every authority and power. [25]For he must reign until he has put all his enemies under his feet. [26]The last enemy to be destroyed is death, [27]for "he subjected everything under his feet." But when it says that everything has been subjected, it is clear that it excludes the one who subjected everything to him. [28]When everything is subjected to him, then the Son himself will [also] be subjected to the one who subjected everything to him, so that God may be all in all.

After a few moments of quiet reflection on the passage, explore the background information found in "Setting the Scene" to provide some context for Paul's instruction.

Setting the Scene

Paul, known as the Apostle to the Gentiles and one of the premier evangelists of the church, traveled throughout the Roman Empire preaching the Good News of Jesus Christ. Sometimes he established Christian communities (as he did in Corinth around the year 51), and sometimes he visited already established communities of faith. Paul wrote letters to prepare the communities for his arrival or to follow up with the believers he had come to know in a given location. Often, his letters were circulated and laid foundations for the developing theology of the church.

Paul wanted the first generation of believers to understand why Jesus' life still mattered even though Jesus was not physically with them, and

he wanted them to understand how Jesus' life impacted the way they lived. Paul's letters and his ideas about Jesus continue to shape us today.

Corinth was a bustling and sophisticated seaport city that, at the time, was a key part of the trade routes from the Adriatic to the Aegean Seas. Not only did goods and services flow through the city, but so did new ideas and cultural influences. Temples to various Greek and Roman gods lined the streets. Schools of philosophy and various religions flourished. Paul's letters to Christians in Corinth were meant to bolster their faith in the one true God, address the growing attempts to meld Christianity with other religious practices, and settle theological and practical disputes that had arisen within the Christian community. A tall order!

Consider how the liturgies of the Triduum (Holy Thursday, Good Friday, and Holy Saturday) pass on to us the most ancient truths about Christ. How do these celebrations help you to enter into events that are now centuries old?

In our excerpt from 1 Corinthians, Paul is reinforcing the heart of the Gospel message that he received and is handing on: Jesus suffered, died, was buried, and then was raised (15:3-11). This Good News is not just an intellectual matter that requires assent; it is the truth that changes our lives and provides a pattern for how we are to live. It not only "wows" those who hear the story but invites them—invites us—to celebrate the Gospel message that out of destruction God brings new life, and out of despair God gives a solid reason to hope.

Just prior to this passage from 1 Corinthians, Paul suggests that denying bodily resurrection in general (as some in Corinth were apparently doing) also denies the bodily resurrection of Christ specifically. He says in 15:14, "And if Christ has not been raised, then empty [too] is our preaching; empty, too, your faith." Paul is adamant in giving witness to the power of God's ability to conquer all things that stand in the way of life, which is a share in God's life here and in the hereafter. Paul challenges those who preach to consistently preach this message of life—whether from pulpits in churches or through the words and actions of all the baptized.

The passage from the First Letter of Paul to the Corinthians will now be explored a few verses at a time. Continue using the questions in the margins to help you apply his words to your own Christian living.

Understanding the Scene Itself

20But now Christ has been raised from the dead, the firstfruits of those who have fallen asleep.

Given the previous section of this letter and Paul's desire to put to rest any doubts about the resurrection of Jesus, we can read the first phrase with this emphasis: "Christ *has* been raised from the dead." For Paul and the first generation of Christians, this is a statement of fact that cannot be denied. Jesus' body was not stolen (John 20:11-16); Jesus has been seen by his followers (Acts 1:3); he has even commissioned them to

It has been said that we aren't to just give our leftovers to God or to God's people in need. We are to give our best: our best selves, our best gifts, our best efforts. God modeled this in giving his Son to us. How does such generosity speak to your own efforts to be generous?

continue his own mission (Matt 28:16-20; Mark 15:16). In the rest of this section, Paul describes what a difference it makes that Jesus, the Christ, is alive and has not been conquered by death. He wants believers to know that their lives should and will be different.

Paul refers to the risen Christ as "the firstfruits of those who have fallen asleep." The word "firstfruits" is a common reference for Paul's audience, especially those who were in any way familiar with agricultural practices over the centuries. It was customary for the first portion of the crop to be given to the owner of the fields being harvested. It then became common for the first portion to be offered to God, who is the ultimate landowner. In the very first book of the Bible, both Cain and Abel offered to God the fruits of their labor, with Abel specifically offering the fatty portion from the "firstlings" of his flock (Gen 4:2-4). Centuries later, when the Hebrew people settled in Canaan, their laws mandated that firstfruits be offered to God (Exod

23:14-16; Deut 26:1-2). The product of the land was sacred, as was the land itself; both were considered gifts from God.

Applying this principle of "firstfruits" to Jesus indicates that he is the embodiment of what God has provided. Just as the best and first harvest is an indication of the quality of the crop to come, so Jesus is the harbinger of what will come for all those who are the product of God's gifts of grace and mercy.

In another letter, Paul describes our hope this way: "If the Spirit of the one who raised Jesus from the dead dwells in you, the one who raised Christ from the dead will give life to your mortal bodies also, through his Spirit that dwells in you" (Rom 8:11).

21For since death came through a human being,
the resurrection of the dead came also through
a human being. 22For just as in Adam all die, so
too in Christ shall all be brought to life, 23but
each one in proper order: Christ the firstfruits;
then, at his coming, those who belong to Christ;

Paul uses an analogy to describe the impact of the resurrection of Jesus in the lives of his followers. It is important to note that Adam, from the Genesis story of creation, is presented here as a prototype of a human being. (*Adam* in Hebrew means "of the earth"; see Gen 2:7.) Speaking of Adam, then, is a way of describing the rebellion of humans against God as told in Genesis 3. When Paul says here and elsewhere (1 Cor 15:45-49; Rom 5:12-14) that sin entered the world through Adam, he is saying that Adam symbolizes the sinful aspects of human nature. In contrast, Jesus embodies the divine image in which all humans are created, so his death and resurrection provide the freedom from sin and death that we desire and have desired since the beginning of time.

In Romans 6, Paul says that we have grown into union with Christ because of grace, and therefore, "If . . . we have died with Christ, we believe that we shall also live with him" (6:8). The good news for us is that just as Jesus took our sins to the cross and grave, he also takes us with him to eternity, where sin and death have no power. This is the consequence of incarnation, of God becoming flesh in Jesus. Paul is saying that what is created—all flesh and blood—matters to God. We are not just spiritual beings who incidentally have bodies. Our bodies, like the body of Jesus, will experience the fullness of life. Jesus is the firstfruits, and his resurrection heralds what will come for us.

It is consistent with Jesus' desire to be one with us that we should desire to be one with him. How have you experienced this longing in the here and now?

**24then comes the end, when he hands over the
kingdom to his God and Father, when he has
destroyed every sovereignty and every authority
and power. 25For he must reign until he has put
all his enemies under his feet. 26The last enemy to
be destroyed is death, 27for "he subjected every-
thing under his feet." But when it says that every-
thing has been subjected, it is clear that it excludes
the one who subjected everything to him.**

We arrive at the ultimate showdown between good and evil. What has begun in the resurrection of Jesus will be completed when all sovereignties, authorities, and powers are subjected to him and the kingdom of God that he proclaims and embodies. In reality, all of these are already under the power of Jesus; they just don't know it yet! What Paul describes, then, is the time when these alternate sovereignties, authorities, and powers acknowledge and submit to the authority of God. In theological language this is called the *parousia*, a Greek term that literally means "arrival" and refers to the second coming of Christ.

What are some ways that we can make clear that the resurrected Jesus is Lord of our lives?

"The last enemy to be destroyed is death." We believe that Jesus has already conquered death, yet each of us mortals will nevertheless face this reality. So is Paul speaking only symbolically of death? No—there are layers of meaning in his use of the word. "Death" refers to the physical end of life (just as resurrection is also physical); it refers to the loss of human dignity through sin; and it refers to rebellious powers opposed to God. Paul testifies that Christ destroys the finality of death and the dread of entering into nothingness. Because of the resurrection of Jesus and the way he conquered the power of death, we are assured that death will have no final authority over us either.

We are living in the time of the resurrection as an ongoing reality until Christ comes again. In this sense, Easter has much in common with Advent, as both seasons remind us to wait in joyful hope. We know this as a time of "already

When has your belief in the promise of the resurrection faltered? What experiences have helped you to accept the deep truth of the resurrection even while knowing that our own deaths are inevitable?

and not yet"—the consequences of all kinds of death are already defeated, but we have not yet experienced this in fullness.

[28]When everything is subjected to him, then the Son himself will [also] be subjected to the one who subjected everything to him, so that God may be all in all.

Throughout this passage, Paul uses the word "when" rather than the word "if." *When* these things happen, as they surely will (having already begun in the resurrection of Jesus), we will also see the complete unity of the Father, the Son, and all creation. Jesus has been given the authority to usher in the kingdom of God, a mission that he shares with us, but that mission is ultimately about uniting creation under the reign of God.

In his ministry, Jesus encouraged those who would listen to "seek first the kingdom [of God] and his righteousness," promising that "all these things will be given you besides" (Matt 6:33). He

modeled for us what "seeking the kingdom" looks like, how that priority in life reflects unity with the Father, and how it leads to a deepening unity with others. Paul seems to be building on that promise by assuring the church that God desires to be "all in all." We are invited into the intimate love shared between the Father and Son.

Living with a resurrection sensibility does not mean that this world and all the relationships it holds are meaningless. Rather, this world and our relationships are all the more important. They are the environment where we learn to live into the promises of our baptism, where we look diligently for signs of God's presence, and where we find evidence of the triumph of life over death. Easter reminds us that the risen Lord gives us reason to hope—for our own resurrection, yes, but also for the seeds of God's kingdom to take root in our midst and for God to bring them to an abundant harvest.

What do your words and deeds illustrate about the God you worship? Do you communicate that God is about life and not death?

Praying the Word / Sacred Reading

In the waters of baptism, we die and are buried with Christ so that we may be raised with him. Through baptism we begin to participate in the risen life of Christ. During the Easter season, there is often a rite of sprinkling when we gather for Mass. Imagine those drops of holy water, reminders of our baptisms, descending on the congregation to wash us so that our eyes see clearly, our ears listen closely, and our hearts are quickened to respond:

Yes, Lord, I do believe.

I believe that your suffering was not in vain, and that your body bears the wounds of our sin so that our sin will not define us.

I believe you defeated the power that death holds over us, and that, as people of life, we too have the strength to conquer all that stands in the way of life because of your grace.

I believe that the world you inhabited is essentially good, and that we are given opportunities each day to bear witness to its goodness in the ways we care for the planet and each other.

Yes, Lord, I do believe.
I believe in your undying love.
I hope in your unending presence.
I believe in you.
I hope in you.

Living the Word

One of the dearest gifts we can share with others is hope rooted in the goodness of God that we experience ourselves. Of course, our lives are sprinkled with sadness, confusion, and even trauma. What we can offer, however, is our testimony to the Lord's companionship through suffering and into life. We need to hear it from others, and we need to share it with others. This kind of sharing in the midst of the real challenges of living is one of the qualities of a vibrant Christian community. Sometimes we have to go out of our way to be a sign of the resurrection.

Contact your parish leaders to find out what kinds of opportunities might be available even in your own parish family. Is there someone who is ill and could use a visitor to offer a meal and some time to listen? Is there a young parent who needs some practical help managing the demands of working and raising children? Are there folks in the neighborhood who could benefit from help around the house? Simply being joyful in giving practical help can become a lifeline for others and a sign of Easter hope when life seems too hard.